The Yoga Spectrum : Exploring the Ancient Wisdom and Modern Applications

By
Professor Manikant Tiwari

Ira Publishers
Kanpur, Uttar Pradesh

ISBN : 978-93-93705-60-0

Fist Edition : 2023

THE YOGA SPECTRUM : EXPLORING THE ANCIENT WISDOM AND MODERN APPLICATIONS

Cover Page : Google | Composing : Printlok

Price : ₹ 130/-

Ira Publishers

405 B, C, Navsheel Jyoti Apartment
127/219-A, Juhi Kalan, Kidwai Nagar,
Kanpur Nagar-208014, U.P., India
e-mail : irapublishers@gmail.com
www.iraimaginations.com
www.facebook.com/irapublisher.in

Preface

Welcome to the world of yoga, where the ancient wisdom of the East meets the modern pursuits of health, well-being, and spiritual growth. In this book, we delve into the fascinating realm of yoga, exploring its science, philosophy, and practical applications. These 15 articles are a collection of diverse perspectives and insights, all aimed at illuminating the multifaceted aspects of yoga and its profound impact on our lives.

From the physiological benefits to the psychological rewards, from the intersection of sports and psychophysiology to the transformative influence of yoga on media and mass communication, this book covers a broad range of topics. Each article offers a unique exploration of a specific aspect of yoga, providing readers with knowledge, inspiration, and practical tools to deepen their understanding and practice.

Acknowledgments

Creating a book like this would not have been possible without the support and contribution of numerous individuals. We would like to express our heartfelt gratitude to all the authors, whose passion and expertise have made this collection a rich tapestry of insights. Their dedication to sharing their knowledge and experiences has enriched the field of yoga and opened new horizons for those who seek the path of self-discovery and personal growth.

We would also like to extend our appreciation to the editors, proofreaders, and designers who have meticulously worked to ensure the quality and readability of this book. Their tireless efforts behind the scenes have helped bring these articles to life in a coherent and engaging manner.

Furthermore, we are grateful to the teachers, gurus, and yogis who have carried the flame of yoga throughout the ages, preserving its ancient wisdom and passing it down to future generations. Their contributions have paved the way for the growth and popularity of yoga as a transformative practice that transcends boundaries of time, culture, and belief.

Finally, we would like to thank you, the reader, for embarking on this journey with us. We hope that the articles in this book inspire and guide you on your own exploration of yoga and provide you with insights that enhance your personal practice and well-being.

May this book serve as a beacon of knowledge and inspiration for all who are drawn to the transformative power of Yoga.

With profound gratitude,

Dr. Manikant Tiwari

Contents

1. The Science and Philosophy of Yoga: Unlocking the Power of Spiritual Practices

Introduction:

Yoga has captivated people around the world with its ancient wisdom and profound teachings. While commonly associated with physical postures (asanas) and breathing exercises (pranayama), yoga encompasses a comprehensive system of spiritual practices. Rooted in both science and philosophy, yoga offers a pathway to self-discovery, mental clarity, and spiritual growth. In this article, we will delve into the science and philosophy of yoga, exploring the benefits of its various practices, and understanding how they can transform our lives.

Section 1: The Science of Yoga

1.1 The Mind-Body Connection:

Yoga recognizes the integral connection between the mind and body. Scientific research increasingly highlights how yoga practices can positively influence the nervous system, hormonal balance, cardiovascular health, immune function, and overall well-being.

1.2 Breath and Pranayama:

Breath is a fundamental aspect of yoga, and pranayama techniques offer numerous benefits.

Controlled breathing exercises induce relaxation, reduce stress, lower blood pressure, increase lung capacity, and improve focus and clarity.

1.3 Yoga and the Brain:

Neuroscience research demonstrates that yoga practices impact brain structure and function. Regular yoga practice stimulatesneuroplasticity, enhances cognitive function, improves memory, increases gray matter volume, and strengthens brain connectivity.

1.4 Meditation and Mindfulness:

Scientific studies on meditation and mindfulness practices show a range of positive effects, including stress reduction, improved emotional regulation, increased attention span, enhanced cognitive abilities, and increased overall well-being.

Section 2: The Philosophy of Yoga

2.1 Ancient Wisdom: The Eight Limbs of Yoga:

The philosophy of yoga is encapsulated in Patanjali's Yoga Sutras, which describe the eight limbs of yoga. These limbs, including ethical principles, physical postures, breath control, sense withdrawal, concentration, meditation, and realization, provide a holistic framework for spiritual growth.

2.2 The Concept of Union:

Yoga means "union" in Sanskrit, emphasizing the aim of connecting individual consciousness with divine consciousness. The philosophy of yoga teaches that we are more than our physical bodies and that true happiness and liberation come from realizing our essential nature.

2.3 Yogic Ethics (Yamas and Niyamas):

The ethical principles of yoga, known as the yamas and niyamas, provide guidance for virtuous living and moral conduct. Practicing honesty, non-violence, self-discipline, contentment, and other virtues helps individuals create harmonious relationships within themselves and with others.

2.4 Mind Mastery and Self-Realization:

The practice of yoga aims at controlling the fluctuations of the mind. Through disciplined practice, individuals can gain mastery over their thoughts and emotions, experiencing a deeper sense of self-awareness and ultimately realizing their true nature beyond the limited ego-mind.

Section 3: Yogic Practices for Spiritual Growth

3.1 Asanas (Physical Postures):

Asanas, the physical postures of yoga, are not merely exercises for physical fitness but also tools for inner transformation. Regular practice of asanas improves physical strength, flexibility, balance, and overall health, while also preparing the body for meditation and deeper spiritual practices.

3.2 Pranayama and Breath work:

Pranayama techniques involve conscious regulation of breath, balancing and harmonizing the flow of prana (life force energy) in the body. This practice helps calm the mind, cultivate vitality, expand consciousness, and prepare for deep states of meditation and spiritual exploration.

3.3 Meditation and Mindfulness Practices:

Meditation is at the core of the yogic journey, facilitating self-inquiry, inner silence, and connection with the divine. Different meditation techniques, such as mindfulness, mantra repetition, and guided visualization, cultivate focus, clarity, and spiritual awakening.

3.4 Karma Yoga and Selfless Service:

Karma Yoga is the path of selfless action and service. By performing our duties and actions without attachment to the results, we cultivate selflessness, humility, and compassion, leading to spiritual growth and a deeper sense of interconnectedness.

Section 4: Applying Yoga Wisdom in Daily Life

4.1 Balancing Work and Personal Life:

Yoga philosophy teaches the importance of finding a balance between work and personal life. Applying concepts like mindfulness, presence, and self-care can help individuals create harmony in their daily routine and promote overall well-being.

4.2 Cultivating Mindfulness and Emotional Intelligence:

The principles of mindfulness and emotional intelligence taught in yoga can be applied in interpersonal relationships, enhancing communication, empathy, and compassionate understanding.

4.3 Ethical Living and Conscious Choices:

The ethical principles of yoga encourage individuals to align their actions with truth, integrity, non-violence, and kindness, promoting a sense of social responsibility and conscious choices in all aspects of life.

Conclusion

Yoga is far more than a physical practice; it is a vast science and philosophy that offers insights into the mind, body, and spirit. Combining the scientific benefits of yoga practices with the profound wisdom of yogic philosophy can help individuals discover their true potential, cultivate inner peace, and embark on a transformative journey of self-realization. By embracing the science and philosophy of yoga, we can find harmony, purpose, and spiritual growth in our lives, leading to a state of lasting well-being and connection with the world around us.

2. Exploring the Depths of Traditional and Modern Yoga

Introduction:

Yoga, an ancient practice originating in India, has gained tremendous popularity in recent years. With its numerous physical, mental, and spiritual benefits, it has captivated people worldwide. Traditional yoga, rooted in ancient texts and teachings, has stood the test of time. However, as society has evolved and the needs of individuals have changed, modern yoga has also emerged. This article aims to delve into the depths of both traditional and modern yoga, exploring their origins, philosophies, methods, and benefits.

Part 1: Traditional Yoga

1.1 Origins and Philosophy:

Traditional yoga finds its roots in the ancient texts of India, particularly the Yoga Sutras of Patanjali. Patanjali's system of Ashtanga, meaning eight limbs, serves as the philosophical foundation of yoga. These eight limbs include principles such as ethical guidelines (yamas and niyamas), physical postures (asanas), breath control (pranayama), and meditation (dhyana).

1.2 Methods and Practices:

Traditional yoga practices emphasize the integration of mind, body, and spirit. Asanas, or physical postures, are performed with proper alignment and conscious breathing, aiming to improve flexibility, strength, and overall well-being. Pranayama techniques invigorate and balance the breath, promoting energy flow within the body. Meditation helps cultivate mindfulness, leading to a sense of inner calm and focus.

1.3 Benefits:

Traditional yoga offers a diverse range of benefits, both physical and mental. Regular practice can enhance flexibility, build muscle strength, improve cardiovascular health, and enhance body awareness. It also aids in stress reduction, promotes mental clarity, improves sleep quality, and cultivates a sense of inner peace and harmony.

Part 2: Modern Yoga

2.1 Evolution and Influences:

Modern yoga has evolved as a response to the changing needs and preferences of practitioners in the contemporary world. It has been influenced by various factors, including Western fitness techniques, scientific research, and innovations in teaching methodologies.

2.2 Varieties and Styles:

Modern yoga encompasses a multitude of styles, each catering to different needs and preferences. Some popular styles include Hatha, Vinyasa, Power Yoga, Bikram, Kundalini, and Yin Yoga. These styles often blend traditional practices with contemporary elements, such as dynamic sequences, music, and variations in intensity and pace.

2.3 Benefits:

Modern yoga retains many of the benefits of traditional yoga, while also catering to specific needs and goals. It can be an effective tool for weight management, improved cardiovascular health, stress reduction, and mental well-being. Moreover, modern yoga places emphasis on accessibility, making it suitable for people of all ages, abilities, and fitness levels.

Part 3: Bridging the Gap

3.1 Incorporating Traditional Principles:

While modern yoga may incorporate innovation and variation, it is essential to maintain the core principles of traditional yoga. Practitioners and instructors should strive to integrate ethical guidelines, mindfulness, proper alignment, and conscious breathwork within modern practices.

3.2 Embracing Modern Advancements:

At the same time, modern advancements can enhance the traditional practice of yoga. Utilizing scientific research, technological tools, and innovative teaching methodologies can enhance the overall yoga experience. These advancements can help deepen one's understanding, enhance physical alignment, and offer personalized guidance.

Conclusion:

Both traditional and modern yoga have their unique merits and contributions. Traditional yoga forms the foundation, with its holistic approach and time-tested philosophies. On the other hand, modern yoga adapts to the needs of the contemporary world, making the practice accessible to a wide range of individuals. By bridging the gap between tradition and innovation, practitioners can experience the rich depths of yoga and reap its profound physical, mental, and spiritual benefits. Whether one approaches yoga from a traditional or modern perspective, the journey to self-discovery and well-being remains profound and transformative.

3. Cutting-Edge Breakthroughs in Yoga and Health

Introduction:

Yoga, an ancient practice originating in India, has been celebrated for its physical, mental, and spiritual benefits for thousands of years. As a form of exercise and meditation, it has gained immense popularity worldwide. With the advancement of technology and scientific research, yoga has witnessed a series of cutting-edge breakthroughs that continue to transform the way we approach health and well-being. In this article, we will explore some of these breakthroughs and their potential impact on the world of yoga and health.

1. Neuroplasticity and Yoga:

Neuroplasticity refers to the brain's ability to reorganize itself by forming new neural connections throughout life. Recent studies have shown that regular yoga practice can enhance neuroplasticity, improving cognitive functions and overall brain health. The mixture of physical postures, deep breathing, and meditation in yoga stimulates the release of various neurotransmitters, such as dopamine and serotonin, which are responsible for mood regulation, learning, and memory. This breakthrough suggests that yoga can be a powerful tool in preventing age-related cognitive decline and even promoting brain regeneration.

2. Yoga for Chronic Pain Management:

Chronic pain affects millions of people worldwide, greatly impacting their quality of life. Traditional medical interventions often involve the reliance on painkillers, which can lead to dependency and various side effects. Yoga has emerged as a non-pharmacological alternative for chronic pain management. Studies have shown that practicing yoga can reduce pain intensity, improve physical function, and enhance psychological well-being in individuals suffering from conditions like fibromyalgia, arthritis, and lower back pain. These findings highlight the potential of yoga as an effective and holistic approach to pain relief and management.

3. Yoga and Heart Health:

Cardiovascular health is a significant concern, with heart disease being one of the leading causes of death globally. Recent research has indicated that the practice of yoga can have a positive impact on heart health. Yoga is believed to lower blood pressure, reduce heart rate, improve lipid profiles, and increase cardiorespiratory fitness. Studies have shown that incorporating yoga into the treatment and prevention of cardiovascular diseases can lead to significant improvements in patient outcomes. This breakthrough paves the way for yoga to be considered as an adjunct therapy alongside conventional treatments for heart health.

4. Yoga for Mental Health:

In recent years, there has been growing recognition of the importance of mental health and the need for effective interventions. Yoga has emerged as a potential breakthrough therapy for various mental health conditions, including anxiety, depression, post-traumatic stress disorder (PTSD), and attention deficit hyperactivity disorder (ADHD). Yoga's combination of physical movement, breath regulation, and mindfulness helps regulate the central nervous system, reducing stress and anxiety levels. Furthermore, the practice of yoga has been shown to enhance mood, self-esteem, and overall psychological well-being.

5. Augmented and Virtual Reality (AR/VR) in Yoga:

Technological advancements have opened up new possibilities for integrating yoga with augmented and virtual reality (AR/VR). AR/VR-enabled yoga experiences offer immersive and engaging practices, enhancing the overall effectiveness and experience for practitioners. Virtual environments can be created to simulate serene and ideal settings, allowing individuals to practice yoga in a personalized and convenient manner. Moreover, AR-powered yoga apps can provide real-time feedback on poses, ensuring correct alignment and reducing the risk of injuries. These advancements have the potential to revolutionize home-based yoga practice and make it more accessible to a wider audience.

Conclusion:

The integration of cutting-edge breakthroughs in fields such as neuroplasticity, pain management, heart health, mental well-being, and technology is propelling yoga into an exciting new era. These advancements have the potential to revolutionize the way we approach physical and mental health, making yoga even more accessible and beneficial for individuals worldwide. As scientific research continues to unfold, it becomes increasingly evident that yoga is not only a timeless ancient practice but a powerful tool for enhancing overall well-being in our modern world.

4. Embracing Yoga as a Pathway to Holistic Living

Introduction:

Yoga, an ancient practice originating in India, has gained immense popularity in recent years due to its holistic approach to health and well-being. Beyond its physical benefits, yoga encompasses a way of life that combines physical postures, breathing exercises, meditation, and ethical principles to promote harmony and balance in all aspects of life. This article explores how embracing yoga can lead to a holistic lifestyle that nourishes the mind, body, and spirit.

1. Cultivating Physical Well-being:

One of the fundamental aspects of yoga is the practice of physical postures, known as asanas, which improve flexibility, strength, and balance. Through a regular yoga practice, individuals can develop a strong, flexible body, prevent injuries, and improve overall physical well-being. The emphasis on proper alignment and mindful movement allows practitioners to listen to their bodies and honor their physical abilities.

2. Nurturing Mental Clarity and Emotional Balance:

Yoga is not simply an exercise routine but also a means to cultivate mental clarity and emotional balance. By incorporating breathwork and meditation into the practice, yoga helps calm the mind, reduce stress, and enhance self-awareness. The focused attention required in yoga allows practitioners to experience a sense of deep relaxation and emotional stability, leading to improved mental health and overall well-being.

3. Promoting Mindfulness and Presence:

One of the key principles of yoga is mindfulness, the practice of being fully present and attuned to the current moment. Through breath awareness and conscious movement, yoga teaches individuals to cultivate a state of mindfulness both on and off the mat. By embracing yoga as a pathway to holistic living, individuals can bring this sense of presence and mindfulness into their daily activities, enhancing their overall quality of life.

4. Developing Spiritual Connection:

Yoga is deeply rooted in spirituality and offers individuals a path to connect with their inner selves and something greater than themselves. Whether it's through chanting, meditation, or moments of stillness, yoga provides a space for introspection and self-reflection. By embracing yoga as a spiritual practice, individuals can tap into their spiritual side, fostering a deeper sense of purpose, connection, and fulfillment.

5. Encouraging Compassion and Ethical Living:

Yoga is not limited to the physical postures; it encompasses ethical principles known as the Yamas and Niyamas. These principles guide individuals towards living a more compassionate and ethical life. The Yamas encourage virtues such as non-violence, truthfulness, and non-greed, while the Niyamas encourage cleanliness, contentment, and self-discipline. By embracing these principles, individuals can cultivate a greater sense of compassion, integrity, and harmony in their relationships and interactions with others.

6. Enhancing Body-Mind-Spirit Integration:

Yoga emphasizes the integration of the body, mind, and spirit, recognizing their interconnection and influence on overall well-being. Through the practice of yoga, individuals learn to listen to their bodies, honor their emotions, and nourish their spirits. By embracing yoga, individuals can develop a greater understanding of themselves and a deeper connection to their own innate wisdom, facilitating a harmonious integration of their physical, mental, and spiritual selves.

7. Fostering a Sense of Community:

Yoga classes and communities provide a supportive and inclusive space for individuals to practice together and learn from one another. Embracing yoga as a pathway to holistic living involves embracing this sense of community and learning from the collective wisdom of fellow practitioners. The connections formed within the yoga community can enhance one's journey towards holistic living by providing encouragement, inspiration, and opportunities for growth.

Conclusion:

Embracing yoga as a pathway to holistic living goes beyond the physical practice of asanas. It encompasses a philosophy and a way of life that nourishes the mind, body, and spirit. By cultivating physical well-being, nurturing mental clarity and emotional balance, promoting mindfulness and presence, developing spiritual connection, encouraging compassion and ethical living, enhancing body-mind-spirit integration, and fostering a sense of community, individuals can fully embrace yoga as a holistic lifestyle. Through this integration, individuals can experience profound transformations, leading to a life of balance, harmony, and overall well-being.

5. Embarking on Spiritual Journeys through Yoga Tourism

Introduction:

In recent years, the concept of travel has evolved beyond seeking adventure or relaxation. As people are becoming more conscious about their overall well-being, they are increasingly drawn towards spiritual journeys through yoga tourism. This unique form of travel combines the ancient practice of yoga with the exploration of new destinations, allowing individuals to nourish their mind, body, and soul. In this article, we will delve into the world of yoga tourism, exploring its benefits, popular destinations, and how it can be an enriching experience for all who embark on this spiritual journey.

1. Understanding Yoga Tourism:

Yoga, originating from ancient India, is a holistic practice that focuses on uniting the body, mind, and spirit through physical postures, breath control, and meditation. Yoga tourism combines the essence of yoga with traditional travel experiences, immersing individuals in the local culture, heritage, and natural surroundings of a destination. It presents a unique opportunity to engage in yoga practices, explore breathtaking landscapes, connect with like-minded individuals, and learn from experienced instructors.

2. Benefits of Yoga Tourism:

2.1 Physical and Mental Well-being:

Yoga tourism offers a multitude of benefits for physical and mental health. By practicing yoga amidst serene environments, individuals can experience improved flexibility, strength, and posture. Regular practice also aids in stress reduction, enhancing mental clarity, and promoting overall relaxation. The combination of yoga and travel allows individuals to escape their daily routine and reconnect with themselves in a tranquil setting.

2.2 Cultural Immersion:

One of the main draws of yoga tourism is the opportunity to immerse oneself in different cultures. Popular yoga destinations, such as India, Bali, Thailand, and Costa Rica, offer a rich tapestry of ancient traditions, colorful festivals, and spiritual teachings. Travelers can participate in local rituals, explore sacred sites, and interact with local communities, gaining a deeper understanding of their customs and beliefs.

2.3 Personal Growth:

Embarking on a yoga tour often leads to personal growth and self-discovery. The practice of yoga encourages self-reflection, introspection, and the exploration of one's inner world. It helps individuals gain a deeper understanding of themselves and their place in the universe, fostering personal growth and self-awareness.

3. Popular Yoga Tourism Destinations:

3.1 India:

India, the birthplace of yoga, attracts spiritual

seekers from around the world. The country's diverse landscape offers various options, from the banks of the holy Ganges River in Rishikesh to the serene ashrams of Kerala. The ancient city of Varanasi and the majestic Himalayas also provide ideal settings for yoga practitioners to delve into their practice.

3.2 Bali:

Bali, known as the "Island of the Gods," is a popular yoga destination offering a harmonious blend of spirituality and natural beauty. Ubud, in particular, is renowned for its yoga retreats, lush rice terraces, and vibrant arts scene. With its spiritual energy, Bali provides an ideal backdrop for yoga enthusiasts seeking inner transformation.

3.3 Thailand:

Thailand's stunning beaches, lush jungles, and tranquil temples make it an inviting destination for yoga tourism. Places like Koh Samui, Chiang Mai, and Phuket offer a wide range of retreats, meditation centers, and wellness resorts. The country's warm hospitality and Buddhist heritage further enhance the immersive experience for travelers.

3.4 Costa Rica:

Costa Rica, with its breathtaking rainforests, pristine beaches, and eco-conscious ethos, has emerged as a sought-after yoga destination in recent years. The country boasts numerous eco-lodges and retreat centers where visitors can immerse themselves in nature, practice yoga, and enjoy sustainable living practices.

4. Planning a Yoga Tour:

Embarking on a yoga tour requires careful planning

and consideration. Here are a few key points to keep in mind:

4.1 Research and Choose a Destination:

Carry out thorough research on different yoga destinations. Consider factors such as climate, cost, local culture, and the type of yoga retreats or programs available.

4.2 Select Accommodation:

Choose accommodations that align with your preferences and budget. Options vary from eco-lodges and boutique yoga resorts to ashrams and retreat centers.

4.3 Find Experienced Instructors:

Look for experienced certified yoga instructors who can guide you through your journey. They will provide valuable insights into the practice and help you deepen your practice.

4.4 Pack Appropriately:

Pack comfortable yoga attire, a reliable yoga mat, and any personal items that can enhance your yoga experience. Don't forget to pack suitable attire for exploring the destination outside the yoga sessions.

Conclusion:

Yoga tourism offers a unique approach to travel by merging spirituality, cultural immersion, and personal growth. By practicing yoga in serene surroundings and exploring new destinations, individuals can rejuvenate their mind, body, and soul. The benefits of yoga tourism extend beyond physical and mental well-being, fostering personal growth, and creating lasting memories. Whether it is embarking on a meditation retreat in the Himalayas or practicing yoga on a beautiful beach, yoga tourism provides an opportunity to embark on a profound spiritual journey unlike any other. So pack your yoga mat, open your heart, and get ready to explore the world while connecting with your inner self through yoga tourism.

6. Unraveling the Psychological and Behavioral Rewards of Yoga

Introduction:

Yoga, a practice originating in ancient India, has gained immense popularity worldwide for its holistic approach to physical and mental well-being. Beyond the physical benefits, yoga is known for its transformative effects on psychological and behavioral aspects of an individual's life. In this article, we will delve into the psychological and behavioral rewards of yoga, exploring the science behind its impact on mental health, emotional well-being, stress management, and behavioral patterns.

I. The Psychological Benefits of Yoga:

A. Stress Management and Anxiety Reduction:

1. Regulation of the Stress Response: The practice of yoga activates the body's relaxation response, reducing the release of stress hormones and promoting a state of calmness. It helps individuals cope with daily stressors more effectively.
2. Anxiety and Depression Reduction: Yoga has shown promising results in reducing symptoms of anxiety and depression. It helps release tension, enhances mood, and promotes feelings of relaxation and well-being.

B. Emotional Regulation and Mindfulness:

1. Emotional Awareness and Regulation: Yoga cultivates self-awareness, allowing individuals to recognize and regulate their emotions more effectively. It provides tools to enhance emotional intelligence and respond to challenging situations with equanimity.
2. Mindfulness and Present Moment Awareness: Yoga encourages mindfulness, the practice of being fully present in the moment. Regular practice enhances an individual's ability to focus on the present, fostering a sense of peace, clarity, and reduced rumination.

C. Improved Cognitive Function:

1. Increased Mental Clarity and Concentration: Yoga incorporates breathing techniques and meditation, which enhance cognitive function, memory, and focus. Regular practice improves attention span and cognitive flexibility.
2. Neuroplasticity and Brain Health: Research suggests that yoga may promote neuroplasticity, the brain's ability to reorganize and form new connections. Over time, this can enhance cognitive abilities, memory retention, and overall brain health.

II. The Behavioral Rewards of Yoga:

A. Self-discipline and Goal Setting:

1. Strengthening of Willpower: The practice of yoga requires commitment, consistency, and self-discipline, helping individuals develop stronger willpower and self-control outside the yoga studio.

2. Goal Setting and Achievement: Setting personal goals, such as mastering challenging yoga poses, provides a framework for cultivating discipline, perseverance, and a sense of accomplishment.

B. Enhanced Self-Esteem and Body Image:

1. Body Awareness and Acceptance: Yoga fosters a non-judgmental attitude towards the body, promoting self-acceptance and appreciation of individual strengths and capabilities.
2. Increased Self-Confidence: The progression and mastery of yoga poses contribute to increased self-confidence and a positive body image.

C. Stress and Emotional Eating Management:

1. Mindful Eating: Yoga encourages mindful eating practices, bringing attention to the body's hunger and satiety cues, reducing impulsive and emotional eating behaviors.
2. Stress Reduction: By reducing stress and promoting emotional balance, yoga can help individuals manage stress-related eating patterns, leading to healthier food choices and enhanced well-being.

D. Relationship Building and Empathy:

1. Cultivating Compassion: Yoga promotes self-compassion and empathy, which extends to interpersonal relationships. The practice helps individuals develop kindness, understanding, and deeper connections with others.
2. Improved Communication Skills: Yoga enhances active listening and clear

communication, allowing individuals to express their needs, boundaries, and emotions more effectively.

III. Integrating Yoga into Daily Life:

A. Establishing a Regular Practice:

1. Consistency is Key: Regular yoga practice is essential to experience the psychological and behavioral rewards. Start with shorter sessions and gradually increase the duration and intensity.
2. Creating a Personal Routine: Tailor the practice to individual preferences and needs. Consider factors such as time of day, location, and choice of yoga styles.

B. Mindful Living:

1. Carry Yoga off the Mat: Bring the principles of mindfulness and self-awareness into daily activities, such as mindful eating, walking, or interpersonal interactions.
2. Integrating Breathwork: Utilize breathwork techniques learned through yoga practice to manage stress, reduce anxiety, and stay present in challenging situations.

C. Seek Professional Guidance:

1. Yoga Instructors: Engage with experienced yoga instructors who can guide and support your practice, providing personalized instructions and adjustments.
2. Therapy and Yoga: Explore the integration of yoga with therapeutic interventions under the guidance of mental health professionals for addressing specific psychological concerns.

Conclusion:

Yoga offers profound psychological and behavioral rewards, positively impacting various aspects of life. From stress management and anxiety reduction to enhanced emotional regulation, self-esteem, and mindfulness, the practice of yoga provides a framework for personal growth and transformation. By integrating yoga into daily life and seeking professional guidance when needed, individuals can unlock the full potential of this ancient practice and experience its transformative effects on their psychological and behavioral well-being.

7. Unleashing the Physiological and Societal Progress of Yoga

Introduction:

In recent years, yoga has gained significant popularity as a form of exercise, relaxation, and mind-body integration. Originating from ancient Indian traditions, it offers a holistic approach to physical and mental well-being. Yoga encompasses various practices, including postures (asanas), breathing techniques (pranayama), and meditation. Beyond its immediate physical benefits, yoga has the power to enact profound physiological changes and drive societal progress. This article aims to explore the physiological and societal progress unleashed by the practice of yoga.

Physiological Progress:

1. Enhancing Physical Fitness:

Yoga postures improve flexibility, strength, balance, and body awareness. Regular practice helps to tone muscles, increase cardiovascular endurance, and improve overall physical fitness. With consistent dedication, practitioners experience increased self-confidence in their physical abilities and are less prone to injuries.

2. Managing Stress and Anxiety:

One of yoga's most significant contributions is its ability to alleviate stress and anxiety. Stress triggers the release of hormones like cortisol, resulting in physical and mental imbalances. Regular yoga practice activates the body's relaxation response, lowering cortisol levels and promoting relaxation. Techniques such as deep breathing and meditation foster a calm and focused state of mind.

3. Improving Sleep Quality:

Sleep disorders have become increasingly prevalent in modern societies. Yoga helps combat insomnia and other sleep-related issues by promoting relaxation and reducing stress levels. Certain yoga poses, such as forward bends and inversions, improve blood circulation to the brain, aiding in better sleep quality and duration.

4. Boosting Immunity:

The practice of yoga enhances the immune system's functionality. The physical postures help stimulate and strengthen the vital organs, ensuring proper functioning. Additionally, deep breathing practices increase oxygen supply to the body, improving overall health and immune response. With a strengthened immune system, practitioners experience fewer illnesses and enjoy better overall health.

5. Balancing Hormones:

Hormonal imbalances can cause a variety of health problems, including mood swings, weight fluctuations, and reproductive issues. Yoga helps restore hormonal balance by reducing stress, improving blood circulation, and activating the endocrine system. Specific asanas like the shoulder stand and fish pose stimulate the thyroid gland, regulating hormone production and metabolic function.

Societal Progress:

1. Enhanced Mental Well-being:

Yoga's impact extends beyond individual well-being, positively influencing society as a whole. By promoting mental well-being, yoga contributes to a happier and more harmonious society. When individuals practice yoga and experience reduced stress and increased emotional stability, it enhances their interactions with others, creating a ripple effect that fosters positive relationships and peaceful coexistence.

2. Fostering Mindfulness and Compassion:

The regular practice of yoga cultivates mindfulness and compassion, enabling individuals to be more aware of their actions and their impact on others. The principles of non-violence (ahimsa) and compassion (karuna) inherent in yoga philosophy encourage practitioners to be empathetic and supportive, leading to a more compassionate society.

3. Enhancing Work Productivity:

Yoga has been embraced by numerous corporations and organizations as it helps improve work productivity. Regular yoga practice reduces stress levels, enhances focus, and boosts creativity. Companies that promote workplace yoga programs witness increased employee satisfaction, reduced sick leave, and improved overall productivity.

4. Creating Health-Conscious Communities:

Yoga studios and community centers play a vital role in spreading awareness about health and well-being. These spaces provide a gathering point for individuals interested in physical fitness and mindfulness practices. Through workshops, classes, and events, yoga communities encourage healthy habits, foster environmental consciousness, and champion overall wellness.

5. Bridging Cultural Divides:

The global popularity of yoga has given rise to a diverse community of practitioners. Yoga brings people from different cultures, backgrounds, and beliefs together, fostering a sense of unity and respect. By transcending national boundaries, yoga acts as a bridge, promoting cultural understanding, and appreciation.

Conclusion:

Yoga's influence reaches far beyond physical exercise; it unleashes profound physiological and societal progress. Through its numerous benefits, yoga enhances physical fitness, reduces stress, improves sleep quality, boosts immunity, and balances hormones. Additionally, it fosters mental well-being, mindfulness, compassion, workplace productivity, health-conscious communities, and bridges cultural divides. As more individuals embrace the practice of yoga, its transformative power will continue to shape society for the better, promoting overall well-being and harmony.

8. The Intersection of Sports and Psychophysiology in Yoga

Introduction:

Yoga, a practice that combines physical postures, breath control, and meditation, has a deep psychological impact on practitioners. Its therapeutic benefits have been recognized for centuries, but more recently, the intersection of sports and psychophysiology in the context of yoga has gained attention. This article explores the connection between sports science and yoga, highlighting the psychophysiological effects of yoga that contribute to enhanced athletic performance, improved mental well-being, and overall holistic growth.

Section 1: The Physiology of Yoga

1.1. Enhancing Physical Performance:

Yoga postures (asanas) facilitate increased strength, flexibility, and balance, which are essential for sports performance. The controlled movements and static holds during yoga sessions help develop functional strength and encourage proper body alignment, reducing the risk of injuries. As athletes integrate yoga into their training routines, they experience improved athletic performance due to enhanced muscular coordination and efficient movement patterns.

1.2. Balancing the Autonomic Nervous System:

The practice of yoga elicits a balance between the sympathetic and parasympathetic branches of the autonomic nervous system, regulating heart rate, blood pressure, and respiration. This enables athletes to achieve an optimal state of arousal during competition, promoting efficiency and focus. The ability to self-regulate physiological responses contributes to better stress management, enhancing the athlete's ability to perform under pressure.

1.3. Enhancing Respiratory Function:

Yoga incorporates various breathing techniques (pranayama) that improve lung capacity, oxygen uptake, and respiratory efficiency. These practices increase the delivery of oxygen to working muscles, reducing fatigue and improving endurance. Athletes who integrate yoga into their training experience enhanced respiratory function, enabling them to sustain effort for longer durations and recover quicker between intense bouts of exercise.

Section 2: Mental Aspects of Yoga

2.1. Developing Mindfulness and Concentration:

Yoga emphasizes being present in the moment, cultivating mindful awareness, and training the mind to stay focused. Through regular practice, athletes develop better concentration skills, allowing them to immerse themselves fully in training and competition. Heightened mindfulness and concentration enable athletes to make split-second decisions, adapt to changingcircumstances, and maintain mental clarity amidst distractions.

2.2. Regulating Stress and Anxiety:

Stress and anxiety negatively impact athletic performance. Yoga's emphasis on breath control and relaxation techniques activates the body's relaxation response, reducing stress and anxiety levels. Athletes who incorporate yoga into their routines experience improved emotional well-being and are better equipped to handle the pressures associated with sports competition.

2.3. Building Mental Resilience:

Yoga involves holding challenging positions and staying present with discomfort. This builds mental resilience and the ability to persevere through physical and psychological challenges. Athletes who practice yoga develop the skills to push beyond perceived limitations, cope with setbacks, and maintain a positive mindset, enhancing their overall mental fortitude.

Section 3: Holistic Growth and Injury Prevention

3.1. Injury Prevention:

Yoga's focus on body alignment, flexibility, and strengthening of supporting muscles helps prevent common sports-related injuries. By addressing muscular imbalances, athletes reduce the risk of overuse injuries and improve their overall biomechanics. The mindfulness cultivated through yoga also helps athletes tune into their bodies, allowing them to identify and address potential areas of weakness orimbalance before they escalate into injuries.

3.2. Faster Recovery and Rehabilitation:

Yoga's gentle movements, stretching, and breathing techniques aid in post-workout recovery and injury rehabilitation. The practice increases blood flow to the muscles, promoting nutrient delivery, and removal of waste products. Additionally, yoga's calming effect on the nervous system reduces inflammation and promotes relaxation, facilitating the body's natural healing processes.

Conclusion:

The intersection of sports and psychophysiology in yoga leads to a multitude of benefits for athletes. Through enhanced physical performance, efficient autonomic nervous system regulation, improved respiratory function, and mental well-being, athletes experience holistic growth. Yoga cultivates mindfulness, concentration, stress regulation, and mental resilience, enabling athletes to perform at their best and recover faster from physical exertion. By embracing yoga as an integral component of sports training and development, athletes can unlock their full potential and experience an enhanced athletic journey.

9. Nurturing Values through Education and the Power of Yoga

Introduction:

In today's fast-paced and competitive world, there is a growing need to emphasize value-based education that not only imparts knowledge but also nurtures moral and ethical values in individuals. Education has the potential to shape the character and outlook of an individual, and integrating the practice of yoga can further enhance this transformative process. Yoga, a centuries-old practice originating from ancient India, offers a holistic approach to physical, mental, and spiritual well-being. Incorporating yoga into the educational framework can cultivate essential human values, creating compassionate and responsible individuals. This article explores the importance of integrating yoga into education as a means to nurture values, foster emotional intelligence, and promote overall well-being.

I. Understanding Value-Based Education:

1. Defining values in education:

Value-based education involves the systematic development and reinforcement of positive personal values in students. It aims to cultivate qualities such as honesty, integrity, empathy, respect, and responsibility.

2. The significance of value-based education:

Value-based education assists in the holistic development of individuals by equipping them to make responsible choices, developing empathy towards others, and promoting a harmonious society.

II. Benefits of Yoga in Education:

1. Holistic well-being:

Yoga offers a holistic approach to well-being by integrating physical postures (asanas), breathing exercises (pranayama), and meditation. These practices enhance concentration, reduce stress, and improve overall physical and mental health.

2. Emotional intelligence:

Yoga teaches individuals to be mindful of their thoughts and emotions. By practicing self-reflection and mindfulness, students can develop emotional intelligence, enabling them to handle stress, conflicts, and relationships effectively.

3. Enhancing focus and attention:

Regular practice of yoga has been proven to improve attention, concentration, and cognitive abilities. Students who practice yoga are more likely to have better memory retention and decision-making skills.

III. Integrating Yoga into Education:

1. Yoga as a subject:

Incorporating yoga as a subject in the curriculum can provide students with practical tools to manage stress, enhance self-awareness, and develop resilience. Yoga sessions can include asanas, breathing exercises, relaxation techniques, and meditation.

2. Mindfulness practices in the classroom:

Teachers can integrate mindfulness practices like brief breathing exercises and moments of silent reflection to help students focus, regulate their emotions, and develop a sense of empathy towards their peers.

3. Yoga and character education:

Character education, aimed at instilling ethical values, can be reinforced through yogic teachings. Yoga philosophy emphasizes values such as truthfulness, non-violence, patience, discipline, and self-control.

IV. Case Studies and Success Stories:

1. Schools implementing yoga-based education:

Numerous schools across the globe have successfully incorporated yoga in their curriculum. Research demonstrates improved academic performance, enhanced emotional well-being, and a reduction in disciplinary issues among students.

2. Personal testimonials:

Highlighting personal experiences from educators, students, and parents who have witnessed positive transformations through yoga-based education.

V. Challenges and Potential Solutions:

1. Resistance to change:

Implementing yoga-based education may face resistance from traditional educational systems and stakeholders. Generating awareness and emphasizing the scientific evidence supporting yoga's benefits can help overcome skepticism.

2. Training and resources:

Educators require adequate training and resources to effectively integrate yoga into their teaching practices. Collaboration with yoga experts and organizations can help provide the necessary support and guidance.

Conclusion:

Integrating yoga into education holds the potential to shape future generations while nurturing universal human values. Through value-based education and yoga practices, students develop essential life skills, emotional intelligence, and a deep sense of self-awareness. By fostering compassion, responsibility, and the ability to make ethical choices, such an educational approach empowers individuals to create a more harmonious and balanced society. It is therefore crucial for educational institutions to recognize the power of yoga and embrace its integration as a means to nurture values in the hearts and minds of learners.

10. Entrepreneurship and Yoga

Introduction:

Entrepreneurship and yoga may seem like completely different domains, but they share striking similarities when it comes to achieving success and overall well-being. Entrepreneurship demands resilience, creativity, and unwavering focus, often leading to stress and burnout. On the other hand, yoga, an ancient practice originating from India, offers techniques to bring balance, clarity, and inner peace. In this comprehensive article, we will explore the profound connections between entrepreneurship and yoga, highlighting how integrating yoga into the lives of entrepreneurs can promote physical, mental, and emotional well-being, leading to greater success in their ventures.

Section 1: The Intersection of Entrepreneurship and Yoga

1.1 The Entrepreneurial Mindset:

Entrepreneurship and yoga both involve developing a certain mindset. Entrepreneurs need to be adaptable, risk-tolerant, and innovative, while yoga cultivates mindfulness, resilience, and acceptance.

1.2 Overcoming Challenges:

Entrepreneurship is riddled with challenges and setbacks. Yoga teaches individuals to face difficulties with equanimity, promoting mental and emotional resilience.

1.3 Creativity and Problem-solving:

Both entrepreneurship and yoga require creativity and problem-solving skills. Yoga practice enhances lateral thinking and fosters a fresh perspective, allowing entrepreneurs to find innovative solutions.

Section 2: Benefits of Yoga for Entrepreneurs

2.1 Increased Focus and Mental Clarity:

Yoga incorporates meditation and mindfulness practices that improve concentration, memory, and decision-making abilities, enabling entrepreneurs to focus on the present moment and make well-informed choices.

2.2 Stress Reduction and Emotional Well-being:

Entrepreneurship can be stressful, leading to burnout and compromised mental health. Yoga's breathing techniques, physical postures (asanas), and relaxation practices relieve stress, promote emotional balance, and foster a greater sense of well-being.

2.3 Enhancing Physical Health and Energy Levels:

Long hours and sedentary work are common in entrepreneurship. Yoga practices, such as dynamic asanas and pranayama (breathing exercises), increase physical fitness, strength, flexibility, and vitality, combating the negative effects of a sedentary lifestyle.

2.4 Harnessing Creativity and Innovative Thinking:

Yoga stimulates the right side of the brain, unlocking creative potential and facilitating innovative thinking. Entrepreneurs who practice yoga regularly often experience enhanced creativity and a fresh perspective, enabling them to develop novel ideas and strategies for their ventures.

2.5 Developing Emotional Intelligence and Leadership Skills:

Yoga cultivates self-awareness, empathy, and compassion, which are essential qualities of effective leadership. Through yoga, entrepreneurs can develop emotional intelligence, leading to better relationships with team members, stakeholders, and customers.

Section 3: Incorporating Yoga Practices into Entrepreneurial Routine

3.1 Morning Rituals and Energizing Practices:

Starting the day with yoga and meditation can set a positive tone, increasing energy levels and enhancing productivity throughout the day. Including practices like Surya Namaskar (Sun Salutation) and energizing pranayama techniques can invigorate the mind and body.

3.2 Mindfulness and Stress Management Techniques:

Entrepreneurs face high-stress situations regularly. Incorporating mindfulness practices, such as mindfulness meditation and breathing exercises, can bring a sense of calm, enabling entrepreneurs to navigate stressful situations with clarity and composure.

3.3 Yoga for Promoting Creativity and Innovation:

Engaging in yoga practices that stimulate creativity, such as restorative asanas, yoga Nidra (deep relaxation technique), and visualization, can activate the creative centers of the brain, enhancing problem-solving skills and fostering innovative thinking.

3.4 Lunchtime Movement Breaks and Desk Yoga:

Entrepreneurs often spend long hours at their desks. Incorporating short movement breaks, stretching exercises, and desk yoga can alleviate physical tension, improve posture, and keep energy levels up throughout the day.

3.5 Evening Relaxation and Rejuvenation:

Wind down the day by incorporating relaxing yoga practices, such as gentle asanas, pranayama, and meditation, to release physical and mental tension, enhance overall well-being, and improve sleep quality.

Section 4: Success Stories: Entrepreneurs and Yoga

4.1 Case Studies of Successful Entrepreneurs:

Highlighting real-life stories of entrepreneurs who have integrated yoga into their lives, outlining the positive impacts it has had on their success, productivity, and well-being.

Section 5: Conclusion - Achieving Harmonious Growth

In conclusion, entrepreneurship and yoga share a mutually beneficial relationship. By embracing yoga practices, entrepreneurs can enhance focus, reduce stress, improve physical health, stimulate creativity, develop emotional intelligence, and lead with authenticity. The integration of yoga into the entrepreneurial journey promotes a state of harmonious growth, leading to greater success, fulfillment, and overall well-being. Remember, finding balance and taking care of oneself is not a distraction from entrepreneurial pursuits; it is an essential catalyst for long-term success.

11. Entrepreneurship and Yoga: A Harmonious Journey to Success and Well-being

Introduction:

In today's fast-paced, competitive world, the demands of entrepreneurship can often leave entrepreneurs feeling overwhelmed, stressed, and disconnected from their well-being. However, a growing trend suggests that incorporating yoga into their entrepreneurial journey can offer tremendous benefits. Yoga, with its ancient roots in holistic well-being, can provide clarity, inner peace, physical strength, and mental focus. In this article, we will explore the beautiful synergy between entrepreneurship and yoga, and how practicing yoga can support entrepreneurs in achieving success while nurturing their overall well-being.

Cultivating Focus and Emotional Balance:

Entrepreneurship demands unwavering focus and emotional balance. Yoga, with its blend of physical postures, controlled breathing, and meditation, can provide the necessary tools to cultivate these qualities. Regular yoga practice trains the mind to stay present, enhancing concentration and attentiveness. Additionally, yoga helps entrepreneurs become more aware of their emotions and develop techniques to manage stress and anxiety effectively, enabling them to make rational decisions even in high-pressure situations.

Creativity and Innovation:

Entrepreneurship thrives on innovation and creativity. Yoga practice taps into the right side of the brain, stimulating creativity and unlocking fresh ideas. By quieting the mind, yoga can help entrepreneurs access their creative potential and find innovative solutions to challenges they face in their business journey. The integration of mindfulness and yoga practice cultivates a receptive mindset conducive to out-of-the-box thinking, thus nurturing an entrepreneurial spirit that can transform ideas into successful ventures.

Self-awareness and Authentic Leadership:

Successful entrepreneurship requires self-awareness and the ability to lead authentically. The self-reflection and introspection encouraged by yoga help entrepreneurs gain a deeper understanding of themselves. Yoga builds self-confidence, enabling entrepreneurs to lead with authenticity and inspire their team. Practicing yoga enhances emotional intelligence, empathy, and compassion towards others, fostering positive relationships and strong networks, which are fundamental to entrepreneurial success.

Stress Reduction and Well-being:

Entrepreneurial journeys can be filled with stress, taking a toll on both mental and physical well-being. Yoga offers numerous physical and mental health benefits, such as improved flexibility, strength, and stamina, along with reduced stress levels. By incorporating yoga into their routine, entrepreneurs can rejuvenate their bodies, calibrate their minds, and find a balance between work and personal life. This holistic approach promotes overall well-being, better decision-making, and sustained productivity in the long run.

Building Resilience and Adaptability:

Entrepreneurs face constant challenges and setbacks, requiring them to be resilient and adaptable. Yoga teaches individuals to face difficulties with resilience, accepting the imperfections and impermanence of life. The physical practice of yoga builds strength and flexibility, mirroring the qualities required to navigate the ever-changing entrepreneurial landscape. Moreover, the mental stamina developed through yoga helps entrepreneurs remain calm and navigate uncertainty, bounce back from failures, and view setbacks as opportunities for growth.

Conclusion:

The ancient practice of yoga beautifully complements the entrepreneurial journey, offering a myriad of benefits to entrepreneurs seeking success and well-being. By incorporating yoga into their routine, entrepreneurs can enhance focus, creativity, self-awareness, and resilience while effectively managing stress and maintaining overall well-being. Through the harmony of entrepreneurship and yoga, entrepreneurs can unlock their fullest potential, leading themselves and their ventures towards greater success and fulfillment. So, roll out your yoga mat, embrace the entrepreneurial spirit, and embark on a transformative journey of balance and growth.

12. Unveiling the Neurological Benefits of Yoga

Introduction:

Yoga is an ancient practice that combines physical postures, breathing exercises, and meditation to promote overall well-being. While it is widely known for its physical and mental health benefits, recent research has also shed light on the neurological benefits of practicing yoga. This article investigates the various ways in which yoga positively influences the brain and its cognitive functions.

1. Enhancing Brain Structure:

Numerous studies have demonstrated that engaging in regular yoga practice can positively impact brain structure. MRI scans have shown that yoga practitioners have greater gray matter volume, particularly in regions associated with attention, impulse control, decision-making, and the regulation of emotions. These structural changes have been linked to improvements in cognitive performance and emotional well-being.

2. Boosting Cognitive Functions:

Yoga has been found to enhance several cognitive functions, including attention, memory, and executive functions. The combination of physical postures, breathing techniques, and meditation works synergistically to increase focus and mental clarity. Research suggests that regular yoga practice promotes efficient information processing and enhances working memory, leading to better cognitive performance.

3. Reducing Stress and Anxiety:

The practice of yoga is well-known for its stress-reducing properties. By engaging in slow, controlled movements and deep breathing exercises, yoga activates the body's relaxation response, relieving stress and anxiety. Studies have shown that regular yoga practice decreases the levels of stress hormones, such as cortisol, while increasing the levels of mood-enhancing neurotransmitters like serotonin. These changes contribute to a calmer, more serene mental state.

4. Improving Mood and Emotional Well-being:

Yoga has shown promising results in improving mood and emotional well-being. By combining physical movement, breath control, and meditation, yoga stimulates the release of endorphins, often referred to as the "feel-good" hormones. Regular practice has been found to reduce symptoms of depression and anxiety, increase feelings of happiness, and improve overall emotional well-being.

5. Enhancing Neuroplasticity:

Neuroplasticity, the brain's ability to form new connections and reorganize itself, is crucial for learning and adapting to new experiences. Studies suggest that yoga promotes neuroplasticity by increasing the production of brain-derived neurotrophic factor (BDNF), a protein that supports the growth and maintenance of neurons. Enhanced neuroplasticity is associated with improved learning, memory, and cognitive flexibility.

6. Balancing Brain Hemispheres:

Yoga practices that involve alternate nostril breathing, such as Nadi Shodhana Pranayama, have been found to balance the activity between the brain hemispheres. This balanced brainwave activity leads to improved cognitive functions and heightened emotional stability. Research suggests that such practices increase alpha wave activity, associated with relaxation and mental clarity, while reducing beta wave activity, associated with stress and anxiety.

7. Promoting Mindfulness and Present Moment Awareness:

Yoga emphasizes mindfulness and present moment awareness, which has a profound impact on the brain. Studies have revealed that mindfulness practices, such as yoga and meditation, increase the thickness of the prefrontal cortex, a brain region responsible for self-awareness, decision-making, and emotional regulation. This increased thickness is associated with improved cognitive functions, emotional resilience, and overall well-being.

Conclusion:

The neurological benefits of yoga are becoming increasingly evident, with research demonstrating the positive impact of yoga on brain structure, cognitive functions, stress reduction, mood enhancement, neuroplasticity, brainwave activity, and mindfulness. Whether you're seeking to improve your cognitive performance, reduce stress, or enhance your emotional well-being, incorporating regular yoga practice into your daily routine may prove highly beneficial. So, roll out your yoga mat and unleash the immense neurological benefits that this ancient practice has to offer.

13. Yoga and Media: Discovering the Intersection of Mindfulness and Mass Communication

Introduction:

In today's fast-paced world, where technology dominates our lives, finding balance and inner peace has become increasingly vital for our overall well-being. Yoga, a practice that originated thousands of years ago, focuses on nurturing the mind, body, and spirit. Interestingly, yoga's principles and teachings have found their way into the realm of media and mass communication. In this article, we will explore the intersection of yoga and mass communication, examining how the practice enhances media professionals' well-being, fuels creativity, and influences the portrayal of mindfulness in popular culture.

1. Mindfulness and Well-being in Mass Communication:

1.1 Managing Stress and Burnout:

The field of media and mass communication is known for its high-stress environment. Journalists, broadcasters, and those working in public relations often face tight deadlines, demanding clients, and emotionally challenging stories. Incorporating yoga and mindfulness practices into their routine can help manage stress, reduce burnout, and enhance overall well-being. Mindful breathing techniques, meditation, and physical postures can promote relaxation, improve focus, and increase self-awareness for media professionals.

1.2 Enhancing Emotional Intelligence:

Media professionals need to navigate a wide range of emotions while interacting with colleagues, clients, and audience members. Yoga fosters emotional intelligence by promoting self-reflection, empathy, and compassion towards oneself and others. This enhances communication skills, conflict resolution, and the ability to establish authentic connections with people.

1.3 Promoting Work-Life Balance:

Yoga encourages individuals to prioritize self-care and find balance in their lives. By implementing mindful practices, media professionals can establish boundaries between work and personal life, preventing burnout and ensuring long-term success. Regular yoga practice helps individuals recharge, improve productivity, and maintain a healthy work-life balance.

2. Fueling Creativity in Media:

2.1 Unlocking the Subconscious Mind:

Yoga and meditation can unlock the subconscious mind, allowing media professionals to tap into their creativity. The practice helps clear mental clutter, silence the inner critic, and promote clarity of thought. Through focused breathing and mindfulness exercises, individuals may experience a heightened state of concentration and inspiration, leading to more innovative and imaginative media creations.

2.2 Cultivating Flow and Mindful Presence:

In media production, the concept of "flow" refers to a state of intense focus and immersion in creative activities. Yoga cultivates this state by increasing present-moment awareness and concentration. When media professionals engage in yoga and meditation practices, they develop the ability to fully immerse themselves in the creative process, resulting in more impactful and authentic content.

2.3 Connecting with Authenticity:

The practice of yoga emphasizes self-awareness and embracing one's true self. This philosophy resonates with media professionals seeking to create genuine and relatable content. By integrating yoga principles into their work, media practitioners can amplify the authenticity of storytelling, making meaningful connections with their audience.

3. Portrayal of Mindfulness in Media:

3.1 Yoga and Wellness Industry:

Yoga's popularity has skyrocketed in recent years, and the wellness industry has capitalized on its widespread appeal. Social media platforms and online influencers have played a significant role in popularizing yoga as a lifestyle choice. The portrayal of yoga and mindfulness practices in the media often emphasizes physical fitness, trendy apparel, and idealized portrayals of serenity.

3.2 Mindfulness in Entertainment:

The depiction of mindfulness in popular culture has become more prevalent, with characters in film and television engaging in yoga, meditation, or other mindful practices. While these portrayals can be positive by raising awareness of mindfulness, they sometimes oversimplify the practice or present it as a superficial trend.

3.3 Responsible Media Representation:

As yoga and mindfulness gain popularity, media professionals have a responsibility to present a balanced and accurate portrayal. By providing a more nuanced perspective on yoga, the media can contribute to viewers' understanding of its true essence. Media producers should strive to portray the holistic benefits of yoga and mindfulness practices, emphasizing their transformative power beyond physical appearance.

Conclusion:

The intersection of yoga and media offers a powerful opportunity for media professionals to enhance their well-being, fuel creativity, and influence the portrayal of mindfulness in society. By incorporating mindfulness practices into their daily lives, media practitioners can manage stress, improve emotional intelligence, and promote work-life balance. The incorporation of yoga principles in media production can ignite creativity, promote authenticity, and foster deeper connections with audiences. However, it is essential for the media to portray yoga and mindfulness responsibly, going beyond superficial trends and highlighting the transformative nature of these practices. Ultimately, the integration of yoga and mass communication has the potential to reshape the media landscape, infusing it with mindfulness, compassion, and a focus on overall well-being.

14. Exploring the Rich Historical Places Related to Yoga in India

Introduction:

India, the birthplace of yoga, is home to a vast array of historical sites that are deeply intertwined with this ancient practice. These sites hold significance as they have served as important centers for spiritual learning, meditation, and the dissemination of yoga teachings throughout history. In this article, we will embark on a journey through time to explore the rich historical places in India that are closely related to the origins and development of yoga. From ancient temples and ashrams to sacred caves and pilgrimage sites, these places offer a glimpse into the ancient wisdom and spiritual heritage of yoga.

1. Rishikesh:

Located in the foothills of the Himalayas and nestled along the banks of the holy Ganges River, Rishikesh is considered the yoga capital of the world. This ancient city has been a spiritual hub for centuries, attracting countless yogis, seekers, and spiritual masters. It is home to numerous ashrams and yoga centers that offer a range of yoga and meditation programs for practitioners of all levels. Rishikesh is also known for its iconic suspension bridge, the Laxman Jhula, which has become synonymous with the yoga experience in this sacred town.

2. Varanasi:

Varanasi, also known as Kashi or Benaras, holds a special place in the hearts of spiritual pilgrims. Considered one of the oldest continuously inhabited cities in the world, Varanasi is a significant center of spirituality, yoga, and meditation. Along the banks of the mystical Ganges River, seekers can find ghats (steps leading to the river) where yoga and meditation practices take place. The city is also known for its traditional music and dance, offering a vibrant cultural experience intertwined with yoga and spirituality

3. Haridwar:

Another ancient city in Uttarakhand, Haridwar is considered one of the seven holiest places in Hinduism. It is famous for the Kumbh Mela, a grand Hindu pilgrimage where millions of devotees gather to take a holy dip in the Ganges. Haridwar is dotted with ashrams and temples where yoga and meditation practices flourished for centuries. The practice of yoga is deeply ingrained in the fabric of this sacred city, and pilgrims flock here to seek spiritual solace and enlightenment.

4. Ajanta and Ellora Caves:

Located in Maharashtra, the Ajanta and Ellora Caves are architectural wonders that have a deep connection to ancient yoga traditions. These UNESCO World Heritage sites feature intricate rock-cut cave temples and monasteries dating back to the 2nd century BCE. The caves depict exquisite Buddhist art and architecture, and some of them even display depictions of yogis engaged in meditation and contemplation. These caves were originally used as retreats for monks and yogis, providing them with solitude and a conducive environment for their spiritual practices.

5. Bodh Gaya:

Bodh Gaya, located in the state of Bihar, is the most sacred place in Buddhism. It is the place where Gautama Buddha is said to have attained enlightenment under the Bodhi Tree. The Mahabodhi Temple complex, a UNESCO World Heritage site, attracts Buddhist devotees from all over the world. Yoga and meditation form an integral part of the Buddhist practices here, with many visitors engaging in these practices to connect with the essence of Buddha's teachings.

6. Hampi:

Hampi, situated in Karnataka, is a treasure trove of ancient ruins that date back to the 14th century. Once the capital of the mighty Vijayanagara Empire, Hampi is now a UNESCO World Heritage site. Amidst the temples, palaces, and sculptures, one can find the remains of ancient yoga platforms and meditation halls. These structures serve as a testament to the profound influence of yoga in the daily lives of the people during that era.

7. Konark Sun Temple:

The awe-inspiring Konark Sun Temple, situated in Odisha, is renowned for its stunning architectural beauty and intricate carvings. Dedicated to the sun god, Surya, this UNESCO World Heritage site features various postures and poses that resemble yogic asanas. The temple's design and sculptures depict the connection between spirituality, nature, and the human body—a theme central to the practice of yoga.

Conclusion:

As we journey through the historical places in India that are deeply related to yoga, we witness the profound impact of this ancient practice on the cultural, spiritual, and architectural heritage of the country. Each of these sites carries the imprints of countless yogis, seekers, and spiritual masters who sought solace, knowledge, and enlightenment through yoga. Exploring these places not only offers a glimpse into India's rich history but also allows us to connect with the timeless wisdom of yoga and experience the transformative power it holds for our mind, body, and spirit.

15. Exploring Career Opportunities in the Field of Yoga

Introduction

The popularity of yoga has been on the rise, with more people recognizing its numerous physical and mental health benefits. As a result, the demand for skilled yoga professionals is growing at a rapid pace. If you are passionate about yoga and want to turn your love for this ancient practice into a fulfilling career, this article will guide you on how to find job opportunities in the yoga field and explore the various career paths available.

1. Teacher Training and Certification

One of the key stepping stones to a successful career in yoga is obtaining the necessary training and certification. Yoga teacher training programs can vary in duration and content, but generally, they cover essential topics such as asanas (yoga postures), pranayama (breathing techniques), meditation, philosophy, anatomy, and teaching methodology. Look for reputable yoga schools or organizations that offer comprehensive and accredited teacher training courses.

2. Yoga Studios and Gyms

Yoga studios and gyms are common places to look for employment opportunities as a yoga instructor. These establishments offer regular yoga classes to a wide range of participants, providing you with the opportunity to gain teaching experience and build your reputation in the industry. Networking within the yoga community and attending yoga events and workshops can help you connect with studio owners and instructors who may be aware of job openings.

3. Corporate Yoga Programs

Many companies recognize the benefits of offering yoga and wellness programs to their employees to improve productivity and well-being. Corporate yoga programs are an emerging market that presents unique job opportunities for yoga professionals. Consider reaching out to corporations, human resources departments, or wellness companies to inquire about teaching yoga classes on-site or as part of wellness initiatives.

4. Health and Wellness Retreats

Health and wellness retreats provide individuals with an escape from their daily routines, allowing them to focus on their well-being. These retreats often include yoga as a core component of their programs. Opportunities to work in retreat centers can involve leading yoga sessions, assisting in organizing retreats, or contributing to the overall wellness experience. Research and keep an eye on retreat center websites or join retreat-related communities and forums to stay updated on potential job openings.

5. Yoga Therapist or Yoga for Special Populations

For individuals interested in a more specialized role, becoming a yoga therapist or working with special populations can be incredibly rewarding. Yoga therapy involves adapting and utilizing yoga practices to help individuals manage specific health conditions or injuries. Completing specialized training in yoga therapy can open doors to work in hospitals, rehabilitation centers, or private practice. Additionally, yoga for special populations focuses on teaching yoga to specific groups, such as children, seniors, pregnant women, or individuals with disabilities.

Conclusion:

The field of yoga offers a diverse range of career opportunities for those who are passionate about sharing the benefits of this ancient practice. By obtaining proper training and certification, networking within the yoga community, and staying updated on job openings, you can find employment in yoga studios, gyms, corporate settings, retreat centers, or even pursue specialized roles such as yoga therapy or teaching yoga to special populations. Cultivating your skills and continuing your education in the field will further enhance your prospects of finding a rewarding job that aligns with your passion for yoga.